Whisk(e

A beginner's a

Dedication

To my wife that always has been there providing her support.

Introduction

Whisky, another drink, right? At least that was what I thought. Yet, while I started digging more into the subject, I find a whole new world.

This book will try to cover through some information related to this magnificent drink and how it has become a favorite in the world. It will serve as an introduction and provide you the reader with information to help navigate the creation of Whisk(e)y. From the origins to production and how three simple ingredients can open a big universe of possibilities.

Finally, it will provide some tips on how to taste and open your palate. Enjoy and cheers!

Origins

Whisky or Whiskey is a beverage that comes from the distillation of fermented cereal grains.

The origin of the name is an anglicized word from the classic Gaelic[1] uisce or uisge (water).

In Ireland and the United States, the word in use is whiskey in Scotland and pretty much everywhere else is known as whisky. In this book, I might use one or the other depending on the context region.

Let's take a look at some historical dates and achievements that have been influential on the drink that we have today.

According to some historians, the distillation has been used since the Second millennial B.C. in Babylonia and Mesopotamia for perfume production. Around 200 A. D, Alexander of Aphrodisias documented the distillation process in which he described how to get drinkable water from the sea.

Glass Alembic - Image by OpenClipart-Vectors from Pixabay

About the year 800 the Arab alchemist Jabir ibn Hayyan, invented the alembic. A glassware apparatus that allowed to distill liquid on a small scale. Some of its designs are still in use in modern chemistry.

The earliest record of alcohol distillation comes from Italy in the 13th century which they learned from the Arabs. The Italians could get alcohol

---

[1] Classical Gaelic was the literary form shared between Ireland and Scotland between the 13th to the 18th century. Later evolved into Modern Irish and Scottish Gaelic.

from distilling wine, even so, they used it as a medicine to treat smallpox and colic. this early stage distilled alcohol received the name of "aqua vitae[2]"
.

Distillation techniques finally came to Ireland and Scotland along the knowledge of producing aqua vitae and the locals starting extracting alcohol from local sources like the grains. The earliest reference to the spirit came from Ireland in 1405 when it is said that it killed a chieftain for drinking in excess in a Christmas celebration. The first reference from Scotland comes from 1494 where malt is sent to a Friar called Jon Cor with an order from the King to produce aqua vitae. As far as we know medicinal purposes were the primary use during that time. King James IV of Scotland was very fond of the drink, and in the process, it became popular among the local population.

Between 1536 and 1541 King Henry VIII of England shut the monasteries leaving a big number of monks without work, many of them transferred their distilling knowledge to the population or created their own distillation business in homes and farms to sustain themselves.

Aqua vitae was primarily used as a stimulant for the harsh winter conditions in Scotland. In those early years of stage, the spirit didn't have any resemblance to the product we have today, it was not a pleasant drink at all. One of the reasons is related to the aging in barrels, which has not been implemented yet. This part of the process provides smoothness and some distinctive flavor of today's whisk(e)y.

In 1608 King James I granted a license to Thomas Phillips to distill whiskey. This license gave birth to the oldest licensed distillery (Old Bushmills in Northern Ireland), even though the distillery itself was founded in 1784. They hold the record as the oldest licensed distillery.

In 1707 came the Acts of Union, merging the crowns from Scotland and England; England already taxed their distilleries, but it was agreed that Scotland won't have to pay that tax. That ended by 1725 with the malt tax which was cataloged by the Scottish as a direct provocation to them. The majority of their economy was based on malt derived products such as spirits and beers. Most of the distilleries were shut down or forced underground. The moonshine name came from that time as most of the whisky was produced at nighttime to avoid being caught.

As England played a major role in the colonization of the New World and with them, Whisky made its way to the Americas. In the thirteen colonies,

---

[2] (Latin for "water of life") is an archaic name for a concentrated aqueous solution of ethanol.

farmers were very fond of the drink and soon they found alternate grains like corn to produce their version. Whiskey was used as a currency during the American Revolution, even George Washington has its own distillery, in Mount Vernon, specialized in Rye Whiskey. During 1791 through 1794 the whiskey rebellion eroded as the new government taxed the production, that fight didn't last long and the new administration succeeded on their plan.

Whisky arrived in India around the 19th century and became popular, opening the first distillery around the 1820s.

In 1820 John Walker started production of their now-famous whisky. This brand, Johnnie Walker, holds today the record of the most popular Scotch Whisky in the world.

Illegal production of whisky in the United Kingdom ended in 1823 after the Excise Act was implemented by the British government, which sanctioned whisky production under the pretense of a licensing fee and a set of payment per gallon, many were given the option to come legally with no repercussions.

In 1823 producers from Old Bourbon County started calling their product "Bourbon".

Thanks in part to the Excise Act, innovation started to ramp up and in 1831 Aeneas Coffey patented the Coffey or column still, which allow distilling whisk(e)y much faster. The Coffey still was not the first design of a column still but it is the most efficient. Others before him like Anthony Perrier and Scott Stein have already developed the basics for the column still.

In 1850, Andrew Usher mastered the art of blending and marketed the whisky to the rest of the world.

Around the 1880s the French industry of brandy and wine was decimated by a phylloxera pest[3]. Whisky became the de facto replacement, helping to boost the industry.

During the prohibition era in the United States (1920-1933), most of the distilleries were crippled, only the production of wine and whiskey for religious and medicinal purposes were allowed. Americans started looking for alternatives and moonshine and illegal market rises. Drink mixers like Ginger Ale and Cola, became very popular primarily used to tame the bad quality of the whiskey available.

---

[3] Phylloxera are almost microscopic insects that feeds on the roots and leaves of grapevines.

Production

Now that we know some history, let's make some Whisk(e)y.

To make Whisk(e)y we will need the following ingredients:

Water, which is considered the most important ingredient among distillers, it should be clean, clear and free from bad tasting influence such as iron. Yeast, every distillery keeps their yeast supply grown in barley malt and kept free from bacterial contamination. And grains, distillers will always try to get top quality grains as they produce a better spirit.

Types of grains

Let's talk about each type of grain and its properties, all these grains have a wide variety of uses besides Whisk(e)y production, like flour, beer, animal food and other types of spirits. These are the traditional grains used for whisk(e)y.

Mixed Grains - Image by DESPIERRES from Pixabay

Barley: This type of grain is grown in temperate climates, is being cultivated for over 10,000 years. Native from the middle east region. It ranks fourth in the type of grains cultivated in the world. It's the signature grain for Scottish whisky.

Corn (Maize): Is the most cultivated grain in the world. Their origins date back around 10,000 years ago in the southern part of modern Mexico. This type of grain is very versatile and has a wider variety of uses than it's counterparts, like Ethanol and oil production for example.

Rye: This is a type of grain can grow in poorer soils than the rest of the other grains, that resistance makes it ideal for cold-weather environment.

Archeological evidence suggests that is being around c. 1800-1500 BCE in modern-day Turkey. Rye has a characteristic sour flavor.

Wheat: This is the primary cereal produced in temperate climates. Cultivation dates back around 9,600 BCE in the Eastern Mediterranean region.

There are some distillers specifically in the United States that are experimenting with other alternatives like:

Oat: They grow better in temperate climates and they have better tolerance to rain than other grains. Oat is highly praised as a healthy choice for food. In the past oat was used to make whisk(e)y, later the use declined, but in recent years some interest has risen. Oat provides the whiskey some grainy aroma and creamy texture. Some brands known to work with oat are Koval and High West.

Rice: Is the favorite cereal for tropical climates. Like corn, their shape is very distinguishable from the other grains. Evidence suggests that rice domestication started over 10,000 years ago in China. Japan is famous to produce spirits from rice, in recent years some distilleries in the United States are starting producing rice whiskey. Flavor-wise they are sweeter than other whiskies. Some recognized brands are Kikori, Fukano, and Vinn.

Millet: it is being cultivated for over 7,000 years primarily in Africa and Asia. They are drought resistant and can be cultivated in semiarid soil. Koval is the only distillery that I know is using this type of grain. The millet whiskey can be cataloged as soft and dry in the palate.

Triticale: is a hybrid between wheat and rye, created in laboratories in the late 19th century in Scotland and Germany. It combines the grain quality of the wheat and the environmental resistance of the rye. Flavor-wise you bet is like a mix between the floral wheat and the spiciness of the rye. Brands using it are Dry Fly's and Corsair.

I'm going to focus on the traditional grains spirits from now on. Here are the steps to produce whisk(e)y.

Malting: The grains obtained are raw and in the case of barley which is used for malted whisk(e)y, it must be treated differently as it has a high amount of starch which needs to be converted into soluble sugar to get the alcohol. To do this, the barley needs to germinate by moisturizing it with warm water for 2 or 3 days. Germination is cut off by drying the product with hot air, normally in Scotland, large ovens powered by peat[4] are used for this purpose and the smoke generated gives their characteristic flavor to the final product. This is the malting process and the final product is called malt. Rye is another grain that can be malted using the same process as barley, but in this case, the name given is malted rye.

Malted Barley - Image by charlieishere@btinternet.com on VisualHunt.com

Preparing the grains: **For other grains besides barley, they are grounded. The meal is then mixed if using multiple grains, and they are cooked in water, which helps to break the cellulose wall that covers the starch.**

Mashing: **Now is when the sugar extraction process can start. The malt or the mixed grains are placed into a large container with warm water. As the water properties can influence the flavor of the final product, most distilleries are close to a river or lake. The grains are constantly moved to help extract the sugars. Even if the distillery is not doing malted whisk(e)y sometimes small amounts of malt are added to help the sugar extraction process. Once as much sugar has been extracted then the fermentation process can start, the resulting mixture is called mash or wort.**

Fermentation: **the fermentation stage starts by cooling down the mix and adding yeast. This process will convert the sugars to alcohol and it will take**

---

[4] Peat is an accumulation of partially decomposed vegetation or organic matter; it is harvested in several countries as a fuel.

about an approximate of 48 hours, some distillers will leave the fermentation for a longer period depending on the flavor profiles they are looking for. Two types of yeast can be used, fermentation with new yeast cells, this method is called "sweet mash process" or previously used yeast strain from a portion of an older batch of mash, this is known as the "sour mash process".

Sour mash is more often used because it's easier to get a consistent mash, making it more effective at room temperature. The low pH[5] will help grow the yeast and avoid bacterial contamination. The sweet mash process requires more maintenance as it has a higher pH that helps propagates bacteria easier, also it has to be in a controlled temperature environment of 80F or 27C for the yeast to propagate better. Some distillers prefer it because allows them to experiment and play with new flavors profiles.

The resulting beer-like liquid often called distiller's beer or wash is between 5-10% ABV[6].

Distillation: The basics of distillation work in the principle that the alcohol boiling temperature (78.3°C / 165°F) is lower than the water (100°C / 212°F). An apparatus called still is used for this purpose. The stills are traditionally made of copper or stainless steel with a copper interior. Copper helps to remove sulfur-based compounds that made the drink unpleasant.

There are two common stills used, Pot stills and Column stills.

Pot stills are the earliest distillation devices, it contains 4 parts:

- Kettle or pot: The wash is heated here.
- Swan Neck: Where the vapor rises and reflux.
- Lyne Arm: Connects the kettle to the condenser.
- Condenser: Which cools down the vapor coming from the kettle and transforms back to liquid state the alcohol.

---

[5] pH is a chemistry scale used to specify the acidity level of a water-based solution. Acidic solutions have a lower pH value.

[6] ABV Alcohol by Volume, a standard measure of how much alcohol is contained in a given volume of alcoholic beverage, expressed as a percentage. In the United States, the measure used is called alcohol proof, which is two times the value of the ABV.

Pot still – Image by Kostya Kakaskind

The resulting liquid is stored in a separate vessel. The amount of alcohol obtained varies depending on the size of the kettle, that's why distillers that use this method perform their work on batch, where the wash is distilled twice or more, depending on the distiller's preference. Between every batch, the Kettle must be emptied and cleaned which can be a long and tedious process. Alcohol levels obtained can get as high as 60% ABV.

The second still is the Column Stills or Coffey Stills, it comprises two columns the first one is the analyzer which has a series of perforated plates.

Column still - Image by Charles Haynes on Visualhunt

The second column is the rectifier which carries the alcohol from the wash and circulates until it is condensed at the desired alcohol level. It behaves like a series of Pot stills one of top of another. Heat is constantly coming from the bottom in the form of steam. The top of the Column is the coolest part, this is from where the liquid is introduced, with the steam interacting with the wash this will vaporize several components causing alcohol and other volatile molecules to rise while the water and solids will go down the column. The lower the remnants go on the column more heat is applied, and it extracts more alcohol. Alcohol goes to the condenser where is cool down and converted back to liquid. Column stills can get up to 95% ABV.

Several factors determine the amount of alcohol, water, and other substances like methanol, acetone, etc. (this is called congeners) in the final product, the temperature of the distillation is one of them. The higher the amount of alcohol in the final product the less flavor will have, as congeners will be eliminated. At 95% ABV, the resulting product will be called neutral spirits; they are used to add more alcohol level to a blend without sacrificing taste. Master distillers try to get a balance on the number of congeners they allow into the final product as too many bad congeners can spoil the flavor on the spirit.

Maturation: Most of the whiskies-whiskeys are aged in wood casks with some exception like moonshine or any other neutral spirits as some of them are used to make cocktails and is preferred a clear spirit for that intent. When a whisk(e)y shows in the bottle label 8 years it means that is the time it passed in the cask before being bottled.

Casks or Barrels are typically made of American and French Oak. Some countries required the use of new barrels, others allow previously used barrels from previous batches and as well other types of spirits or even further from non-distilled drinks like wine. Charred barrels are common, this is a technique used mostly in American Whiskey where the inside of the barrel is burned, this allows to have some caramel-like flavor and darker color on the final product.

Barrels are stored in warehouses. Normally water is added to reduce alcohol content about from 50% to 60% in American Whiskey and 65% or more in Scottish Whisky, why the difference you might ask? The simple answer is temperature. In Scotland, the barrels are stored in a cool, wet environment and they absorb water so the spirit will have less alcohol content at the end of the maturation process. In the United States, the temperatures are usually higher and have drier conditions, and this will make the spirit to lose water levels.

Whiskey Barrels - Image by skeeze from Pixabay

During this time the flavors of the spirit combine with natural compounds in the wood barrel. The wood is an absorbent surface, and that allows the alcohol and the water to move in and back between the pores, likewise, the barrel gets the influence from the environment where it is stored. Air quality, temperature, and humidity will influence the flavor of the product.

The reason Oak is the preferred wood for making the barrels is that is one of the few woods that won't leak. These properties were said to be first discovered by the Roman Empire when conquering Gaul as they noticed that locals used it to transport beers and meads. The Romans find out that the Oak was easy to bend and that it has waterproof properties to help preserve their wine. With time the Romans starting noticing that the wine stored in the wood barrels will have better taste than the one preserved on clay amphoras, which was the standard way before.

Blending: The majority of whiskies-whiskeys are blended. The primary goal of this process is to create something new, joining different batches and trying to get a harmonious balance of flavor. Every single Whisk(e)y used for the blend has its characteristic profile, the Master blender will try to highlight some of those profiles more than others. When the blending process is completed, then the product is sent to bottling or sometimes could be sent back to barrels to age a little more time, it all depends on what the distiller wants to accomplish. Based on location and type of spirit caramel coloring can be used during this stage.

Packaging: Glass bottles are the standard to store the product once it is ready for consumption as it doesn't change the color or the taste of the whisk(e)y. They bottle the product with a minimum of 40% ABV. The spirit can be diluted with water at this stage to reach a desirable alcohol grade.

?

Whisky bottle - Image by Waldrebell from Pixabay

Types of whisk(e)y

Identifying the type of whisk(e)y, might seem overwhelming for a neophyte. In general, we have malted whisk(e)y which is primarily made of malted barley and we also have grain whisk(e)y which is made from other grains that have not passed through the malting process. This information, however, might not be properly labeled in the product, here are the main categories you will find on the label of the product.

Single Malt: made in one distillery that uses only malted barley. Single malts share a roast, toffee-flavored cereal quality as a benchmark characteristic, other flavors might show up depending on style and location. Most people assume that single malt is only produced from one batch, this is not the case. It could contain different single malt batches produced in the same distillery for several years. The year specified in the bottle is the youngest batch. This is done to have consistency in flavor in the final product and to achieve the distillery signature taste.

Blended Malt: a mixture of single malt from different distilleries. The same rule about age applies here, the year of the younger batch is the age displayed in the bottle.

Blended: a mixture with different types of whiskies-whiskeys that may or may not come from different distilleries. Blending is almost like another form of art where a master blender will mix several batches from different products to get the right zest. They often add some neutral spirits to the mix and small amounts of sherry and/or port wine to help blend the flavor better.

Cask Strength or Barrel Proof: most of the whiskies-whiskeys are diluted with water to reach a percentage of around 40% ABV making them more appealing for drinking. When a product comes with this label, it means that it is bottled directly from the barrel with little or no dilution. These are rare and usually more expensive.

Single Cask or Single Barrel: when the product comes from a single barrel, usually is displayed in the bottle. The taste can vary on whisk(e)y from the same batch with different cask. This is a premium class, and each bottled comes marked from which specific barrel they came from.

Types by country/region

Scotland

Scotland has a long tradition of making whisky and they take their business very serious. The Whisky that is produced in Scotland is often called Scotch.

Eilean Donan Castle, Scotland - Image by E. W. Forbess from Pixabay

To be considered a Scotch the distillers must adhere to some regulations. To name a few:

- Produced entirely in Scotland.
- Alcohol must be made from malted barley.
- Aged for no less than 3 years in an oak cask.
- Distilled at a maximum strength of 94.8% ABV.
- Must have a minimum of 40% ABV.
- No added substance added other than water and caramel colorant (E150a[7]).

---

[7] E150a is a water-soluble food coloring, used primarily because doesn't change the flavor of the spirit.

Scotland Whisky Regions

Scotland has five regions that produce whisky, each one provides different characteristics of taste profiles.

Lowlands: few distilleries are left on this region, Whiskies from this area tend to be lighter and smooth. At one point in history, all the whisky produced here was triple distilled. Some known distilleries are Bladnoch, Glenkinchien, and Aushentoshan.

Highlands: this is the biggest of the regions and flavor profiles are very diverse. If we can group them on a profile, we can catalog them as light, fruity and spicy. Highlands account for 25% of the malt produced in Scotland. Some distillers in this area are Dalmore, Glenmorangie, and Glengoyne. Some experts are starting to use an extra region derived from the highlands called the Islands, which is basically all the islands surrounding the Highlands region, some distilleries from the Islands are Highland Park and Talisker.

Islay: the smaller region, not to be confused with the Islands sub-region, well known for producing peaty and smoky tastes, the flavor profile might lean to salty, as sea surrounds them. Some historians believe that the distillation process arrived at Scotland from Ireland through here when the Lord of the Islay married the daughter of an Ulster[8] Baron. Some distilleries from this region are Ardbeg, Laphroaig, and Lagavulin.

Speyside: half of the distilleries in Scotland are in this region. Even that it is a small geographical area it accounts for over 60% of malt production in Scotland. Flavors are more complex and richer with sweet notes. Some distilleries here are Glenfiddich, Macallan and Glen Moray.

Campbeltown: only three producers remain on what once was a famous region. This area displays a resemblance flavor profile to Islay with heavy influence from the sea. Springbank and Glen Scotia are distilleries in this region.

Scotch can be categorized as well into.

Single Malt: only malted barley and water is used from a single distillery using pot stills. Glenmorangie, Caol Ila and Tamdhu are distilleries that produce single malt.

Single Grain: this whisky can have a mix of grains besides malted grains. The term single, in this case, means that it is only one distillery. Most of the single grain will be used to produce blended whisky. Some distilleries that produce this type are Girvan, Cameronbridge, and Cambus.

Blended Malt (Vatted Malt or Pure Malt): a mixture from at least two single malt whiskies from different distilleries. This blend might contain single malts of different ages. Some examples of blended malt are Johnnie Walker Green Label and Monkey Shoulder.

Blended: most whiskies produced in Scotland are blended. Producers blend different types of whisky to make a distinctive flavor that represents the brand. Some examples are Chivas Regal, J&B and Dewar's.

Scotch has a distinctive smoky flavor that comes from the malt heated over a peat fire oven, which adds some oily and acrid properties to the malt. The variation of flavor between the different Scottish regions can be attributed partly to the amount of heat the malt receives.

Ireland

Ireland has an equally long if not longer whiskey tradition than Scotland. Usually, the whiskey is distilled three times. This technique produces a

---

[8] Ulster is a region located in the north part of Ireland.

smoother drink, meaning that the flavor provided by the grains will be more subtle.

Ireland dominated the whiskey world in the 19th century, but Scotland fought back by buying and closing some distilleries in the region, basically crushing the competition. Later the Irish independence war came, wounding the whiskey industry and leaving just a few distilleries open on the north side. Irish whiskey has lost some ground but lately is regaining some momentum which is a good thing for us, the consumers.

Country house, Ireland - Image by wagrati_photo from Pixabay

Flavor profile in Irish Whiskey is very diverse but if we can simplify, it can be described as lighter compared to Scotch, with fruity notes and less peaty and smoky.

Here are some prerequisites:
- Distilled and aged in Ireland.
- Distilled at a maximum strength of 94.8% ABV.
- Must have a minimum of 40% ABV.
- Alcohol must be made from yeast-fermented grains.
- Aged for at least 3 years in wooden casks.

We can also classify Irish whiskey as:

Single Malt: like its Scotch counterpart, single distillery using single malted barley, usually triple distilled. Some single malts to name some are Bushmills, Tyrconnell, and Connemara.

Single Pot still: a mixture from malted and unmalted barley distilled in a pot still on a single distillery. This style is unique to Ireland. It's said to produce a thicker texture and spicy flavor. Some whiskeys on this style are Redbreast, Midleton, and Green Spot.

Grain: made from a variety of grains in a column still. Usually lighter and containing neutral flavors. The vast majority of them are used to produce blended whiskeys. Some examples are Teeling Single Grain and Egan's Vintage.

Blended: like Scotch whisky, the majority of Irish whiskey is blended. It's a combination of all styles above. Some recognized brands are Jameson, Tullamore, and Fercullen.

United States

The vast geography of the United States has allowed them to produce different whiskeys, which depending on the region they can develop very distinctive flavor profiles. But in general, American Whiskeys are sweeter and less smoky than their counterparts in Scotland and Ireland.

Barn in Kentucky, USA - Image by Amy Reed on Unsplash

These are the United States Whiskeys categories and their federal regulations:

Straight: is a whiskey that has been aged for at least 2 years in new charred oak cask. It has not been mixed with any other spirit and has not used any colorant or additive. Mixtures of straight whiskeys are allowed as long as they are from the same state, if not they must be called blended straight whiskeys. Also, it cannot be distilled to over 160 Proofs (80% ABV).

Light: this whiskey can be stored in used or uncharred new oaks casks, and distillation needs to be higher than 160 proof. This is ideally used for mixing cocktails. Some examples are High West Light Whiskey and Slaughterhouse.

Spirit: a mixture created from neutral spirits[9] and they must contain at least 5% of a proof gallon basis whiskey (straight whiskeys or a combination of whiskeys if the straight whiskey is used at less than 20%). The flavors fluctuate a lot depending on the combination used, some brands are American Spirit and Whippersnapper Whiskey.

Blended: a mixture that contains straight whiskeys or any blend of straight whiskeys containing not less than 20% of straight whiskey and, separately or in combination other whiskeys or neutral spirits. Some brands are Smooth Ambler Old Scout and Griffo Stony Point.

Whiskey Types:

Bourbon: This is the most recognized type of American Whiskey. Should be made with at least 51% Corn-mash based. It was first produced in Bourbon County in Kentucky, that's where the name comes from. Must have a minimum of 80 proofs (40% ABV), has no aging requirement but if aged it has to be on new charred oak casks. Flavor profile tends to be sweeter than Scotch, we can perceive also robust flavors of vanilla and maple syrup. With aging, you get some leathery hints, like in the case of the straight bourbon. Some names that come to mind are Four Roses, Evan Williams and Maker's Mark.

- *Tennessee:* while not technically recognized as a category, their brands are known worldwide. It is a straight bourbon produced in the state of Tennessee. It differs from bourbon due to a filtration method using maple charcoal chips (ricks), before it reaches the aging process. This procedure changes the chemistry of the drink and the resulting whiskey will be more soft and

---

[9] Neutral spirits: they can be made from about anything, from grains, sugarcane and different types of fruit. They are distilled with a high alcohol content about 95% ABV.

mellow compared to Bourbon. Some known names are Jack Daniels and George Dickel.

Corn: should contain at least 80% of corn. It doesn't have to be wood-aged like Bourbon, however, if maturation is done, it has to be finished on an uncharred oak barrel and lower than 125 proof. Some recognized brands are Midnight Moon and Ole Smoky.

Rye: the same rules apply as Bourbon but should be made with at least 51% Rye-mash based. Traditionally linked to the northeast states. Flavor profiles are spicier and fruitier than Bourbon. Some brands are WhistlePig, Old Overholt and Templeton Rye.

Wheat: identical as Rye and Bourbon but containing at least 51% Wheat-mash based. Flavor profiles are more floral and lighter than Bourbon. Some recognized brands are Bernheim Straight and OYO Oloroso.

Malt and Malted Rye: similar to the others before but containing at least 51% of malted Barley or malted Rye. A recognized brand is Woodford Reserve's Straight Malt.

- *American Single Malt:* is a fast-growing trend in the industry using 100% malted barley. Like their Scotland and Ireland counterparts, they are produced on a single distillery. They are relatively new, and the Federal Government has set no regulations yet, so they fall under the category of Malt Whiskey. Flavor profiles are smoky, aromatics and honey-like. Some known brands are Balcones Single Malt and Hillrock.

Canada

Canadian whisky is also known as Rye Whisky,[10] started being produced somewhere in the 19th century. They are lighter and smoother compared to Scotch.

Most of the Canadian Whiskies are blended and can contain corn, rye, wheat, and barley malt, with corn typically the predominant ingredient. Unlike the United States, the grains are not mixed before the mashing process, the whole procedure is made separately for each type of grain and they blend the resulting spirits before the bottling or during the aging process.

---

[10] Canadian Whisky is known as Rye Whisky because when distillers started operating in the country the only grain that could survive the harsh winter conditions was the rye. The name got stuck even if the amount of rye used is small compared to other grains.

A little known detail is that Canada was the first country that passed legislation requiring that whisky must be aged, which was in the year 1890. In fact, the Scotch legislation in 1916 is modeled after the Canadian law.

During the United States prohibition era, Canadian whisky was smuggled through the Detroit River, which got to be known as the river of booze.

Moraine Lake In Alberta, Canada - Image by David Mark from Pixabay

Here are some regulations:
- Mashed, distilled and aged in Canada.
- Must be aged for at least 3 years in wooden barrels.
- Minimum of 40% ABV.

Some recognized brands are Crown Royal, Canadian Club, and Seagram's.

Japan

Japanese Whiskies are capturing attention in the world. They are compared to Scotch whiskies from the Speyside and Lowland Regions. They produce single malt and blended.

Two names can be linked to the origins of Whisky in Japan, Masataka Taketsuru and Shinjiro Torii. In 1918 Taketsuru traveled to Scotland to learn their techniques. When he returned to Japan, he joined with Torii a pharmaceutical wholesaler. Taketsuru's dream was to set a distillery on Hokkaido because he thought the landscape had the most resemblance with Scotland, however, Torii wanted to have a distillery closer to a big market site and he builds the distillery in Yamazaki, in the suburbs outside Kyoto, in 1923. Some years later, Taketsuru left the company and build his distillery on Yoshi, Hokkaido, in 1934. Eighty years in the future the companies founded by Torii and Taketsuru (Suntory and Nikka respectively) still dominates the Japanese whisky industry.

Chureito Pagoda and Mount Fuji, Japan - Image by Walkerssk from Pixabay

The following countries have a young industry, or they have not developed full potential yet. Most of them are not known in the international market.⏵

Australia

Australia is a newcomer in the industry. Distilleries starting opening around 1992 around the south part of the country with a large portion of them on the island of Tasmania.

Australian whisky is starting to get attention worldwide with some brands winning international awards. Some of the well-known brands are Lark and Sullivan's Cove.

England

They have a tradition of whisky with reference dating back to the 1800s. However, industry was decaying and their last distillery remaining closed down in 1905. In 2006 in Norkfold the first whisky distillery in about 100 years opened. They are producing excellent spirits, now we can see more distilleries starting to show up and as of today, they are already more than ten. Some recognized brands are the English and Steel Bonnets.

Germany

Germany is known worldwide for its beer excellence. Their barley quality is also praised. One might think that they should be developing whiskey for a long time, but they started about 30 years ago. Some known brands are Slyrs and Stork Club.

India

Whisky was introduced in India around 1820. They have several distilleries that supply the local market. A large number of them work with several types of grain and then blend the product with alcohol made from molasses, this disqualified them to be recognized as whisky in the international market. There are few distilleries that produce proper whisky. Barley is harvested in the north part of the country but the majority uses malt imported from Scotland. Amrut and Paul Jhon are recognized brands.

Czech Republic, Denmark, Finland, France, Georgia, Italy, Netherlands, Spain, Sweden, Taiwan, Russia, and Wales complete the list, all of them with very few distilleries.

Chemistry and flavor profiles

Like other distilled drinks whiskies-whiskeys are very complex beverage with a wide range of flavoring compounds. There are over 200 detected after chemical examination. Here are the compounds that make a Bourbon taste different than a Scotch.

Phenolic Compounds: Phenols contribute to the smoky flavor and bitterness. For example, in the Scotch, the phenolic compounds are acquired when drying the malt using peat smoke. Other phenolic compounds come from the use of charred oak casks in the aging process. Phenol, cresols, xylenol, and guaiacol are the main phenolic compounds found in the whisk(e)y, medicinal aromas originate from them.

Aldehydes: There are different aldehydes. Some of them originate from the oak barrel and they provide a range variety of flavors like spiciness, woody aroma, vanilla tone, grainy and herbal flavors. Many aldehydes (acetals) are created on the fermentation process and even though most of them are lost during the distillation, a few will remain. Some Aldehydes that can be named are syringaldehyde, coniferaldehyde, sinapaldehyde, and hexanal.

Esters: They give the whisk(e)y the fruity flavors and aromas. Sweet apple and banana-like are common. Several Esters are formed during fermentation from the combination of fatty acids and alcohol. Many whiskies-whiskeys are chill filtrated which eliminates the esters as their presence might cause some cloudiness appearance in the product. Some Esters to name a couple are ethyl-hexanoate and isoamyl acetate.

Whisk(e)y Lactones: Lots of compounds are imbued to the spirit through the aging process this is the case for the whisk(e)y lactones which provide spicy and coconut-like flavors. They are isomers[11] of each other and usually, these are found cis- and trans-3-methyl-4-octanolide. They originate in the wood barrels where the spirit is aged.

Other Compounds: several other compounds influence the whisk(e)y with a wide range of flavors and aromas. This could happen by different

---

[11] Isomers are molecules with identical formula, but distinct structure.

factors like the environment where the barrels are stored, and the water used during the distillation. Some common tonal flavors are floral, buttery, burnt, rubber-like, metallic and meaty. Many of these composites can include not desirable ones like those that provide sulfur-containing compounds, which their presence can be eased by using copper stills. Some known compounds are phenylethyl alcohol and Diacetyl.

Health effects

There are a lot of studies related to alcohol and its effect on us and while many of them are not conclusive there's no denying that there are some benefits that can be measured.

One shot of whisk(e)y contains about 108 calories, comparing to another drink a pint of beer has around 204.

According to some research, whisk(e)y can act as a blood thinner which can reduce the risk of heart attacks. The consumption of alcohol in moderate amounts can boost the HDL cholesterol (the good one, which helps remove the bad cholesterol that accumulates in the arteries).

Whisk(e)y can help ease the common cold symptoms. In several countries is mixed with some home-made remedies, and with its antibacterial properties, it can help combat throat infections.

Speaking of antibacterial properties. Whisk(e)y can help cleaning any type of wound in case you don't have any first aid kit around, helping to prevent the growth of bacterias. It's also well known that alcohol helps alleviate pain.

It can help control diabetes. Higher consumption of alcohol might increase sugar levels in the blood, but in moderate amounts produces a contrary effect.

Whisk(e)y contain the same antioxidants found in wine in a larger amount like the Ellagic[12] acid, which helps prevents the formation of cancer cells.

There are lots of other studies on which they show that drinking alcohol in moderate amounts can be beneficial, like reducing the risk of dementia, improve libido, lower risk of gallstone, increase immunity and reduce stress, among others. Just like every type of food, moderation is the key.

---

[12] Ellagic Acid is a natural phenol antioxidant found in several vegetables and fruits especially in walnuts, strawberries, raspberries, pecans and grapes.

How to drink Whisk(e)y

Will make it easy for you, any way you like it, either neat, with ice, water or mixed with something else to make a cocktail.

Let's say that you want to try a new whisk(e)y and will like to get a full spectrum of aroma and flavor, here are some of my recommendations.

It is better to use a tulip-shape glass, also called Copita[13] or Sherry glass, regularly used for wine. The shape allows the aroma of the drink to be truly appreciated as it narrows down the stream directly to the nose while keeping it away from the drink. We have similarly the Glencairn[14] cup, it has all the pros of the copita glass in a shorter body.

So what to do to appreciate the whisk(e)y, pour a little into the cup, check the color by lifting the cup through the light. Have in mind that some types of whiskies allows the use of caramel coloring. Not the case of American straight whiskeys, color can be appreciated as they don't allow any artificial enhancement. Lighter crystalline colors are associated with younger whiskeys, while darker caramel colors are linked with older ones.

Now that you have seen the spirit color let's use your smell sense. It is a good idea to take it slow to allow your nose to adapt to the alcohol, get some gentle breath by waving the cup close to your nose, repeat a few times. You can swirl the cup if you like, that helps aerate the spirit and brings up more compounds. Every time you smell you will get more scents and when your nose feels more comfortable with the alcohol, you can leave it for a longer time on the cup.

Now let's taste the spirit. Take a small sip and let it rest on the tongue for a moment, then chew the whisk(e)y a little, move it forward and backward gently and to the sides, and then swallow to see how it ends on the palate. Try to recognize some flavors. After a couple of sips, you can try adding a bit of cool water, like a few drops from a spoon or using a straw grabbing some water from another cup. If the whisk(e)y has a high ABV percentage you might need to add more water. Some experts say that the best level of appreciation is between 35% ABV to 40% ABV, but you decide how you like it or feel comfortable with it. The water turns down the alcohol level and allows you to recognize some aromas and flavor profiles covered by the alcohol.

---

[13] Copita glass it has an aroma-enhancing narrow taper that makes them great for nosing and tasting. They are tall in size.

[14] The Glencairn cup was designed with the help of 5 Whisky Masters distillers in Scotland. The shape resembles the copita glass in a smaller body size.

This is the elegant or fancy way to taste a new whisk(e)y, but sometimes it might not be the best technique because it all depends on the occasion and the mood. Let's say, that you are in a bar with some friends and you don't want to look like a snob, here are some advises to get some flavor profiles from the spirit. When you order the whisk(e)y avoid asking ice at least initially, order a neat drink to try it, check if the flavor profile is something you like. If you detested it, don't discard it yet, add some water and try it that way. While whisk(e)y on the rocks might sound cool is not necessarily the best way to appreciate the spirit. Ice numbs your palate and might dull the flavors. But like I said earlier is always a personal choice so if you love ice with the whisk(e)y go for it, I'll commend using big blocks as they dilute slower.

If you are just starting to be familiarized with the whisk(e)y, go for something smooth first, that way your palate gets used to the taste. You can try for example a bourbon, a wheat whiskey or a blended whisk(e)y.

If you have tried and still don't like it mix it, there are many whiskies-whiskeys cocktails and most likely you will find something that you will like.

I've been drinking many types of spirits, liquors, beer, wine, etc... I was not a fan of the whisk(e)y, it started growing on me after I was introduced to a cocktail (Old Fashioned). One day at a local bar they offered me their specialty which was an Old Fashioned and since that day my mind was blown away. I have never tasted an old-fashioned cocktail with such flavors. I had to ask what was inside this drink, what they use besides the regular ingredients on the Old Fashioned. The flavors profile I was getting were, spicy, smoky, coffee and tobacco-like, remind me of a barbecue. Turns out that they were just using the regular ingredients the only alteration was the spirit they were using. The whiskey in question is the Balcones Brimstone, which has one of the most dividing flavor profiles for whiskey lovers, is just like Dr. Pepper either you love it or hated it. Somehow my drinking senses have been enhanced after tasting this whiskey. I can sense more flavor profiles whereas before I didn't notice or cared, not only with Bourbons but also with Scotch. Whisk(e)y has been growing in me ever since and I just needed to know more about this great drink and start trying new ones whenever possible.

Before my "awakening" I was given a bottle of a Scotch from Lagavulin. I tried and I didn't like it at all, to me tasted like plastic or rubber. Forward back to today, I love this Whisky and I keep coming back for more. I can feel the saltiness and herb-like flavor, that plastic flavor has been transformed into smoke.

Drink appreciation and with this, not referring only to whisk(e)y, is not something you are born with, it takes some time to develop. As you get older your palate also changes. The more you try different types of spirits you will be developing more your senses.

Don't get too excited and try to drink all you can. Life is always a constant battle to get the right combination and in the drinking world, moderation is always the key.

Whisky Decanter and three cups - Image by Victor Hughes on Unsplash

Cocktails

Whether you don't like the experience of drinking neat spirits or will like to get rid of some whisk(e)y you don't like, or just want to experiment with new drinks with your favorite whisk(e)y.

Here are some of my favorites cocktails you can make. Some of these ingredients can be interchangeable.

Manhattan: **Legend says it was invented at the Manhattan Club in New York, around the 1870s, it was invented by Dr. Iain Marshall in a banquet hosted by Lady Randolph Churchill, mother of prime minister Winston Churchill. Other references mentioned that it was invented by a bartender named Black in a bar on Broadway in the 1860s.**

Ingredients:

2 oz of Whiskey (best with Bourbon, Rye or Canadian Whisky)

1 oz of sweet Vermouth[15].

2 or 3 dashes of bitters[16].

1. Add all the ingredients to a mixing glass with ice and stir until well-chilled.
2. Strain into a cocktail[17] glass.
3. Garnish with a cherry.

---

[15] Vermouth is a fortified wine, meaning that has some distilled alcohol to increase ABV levels. It is flavored with herbs and spices, it comes in two formats: sweet and dry.

[16] Bitters are used to flavor cocktails. They contain alcohol and usually are made from botanical matter, they impart some bitter, sour and sweet flavor to the cocktails.

[17] Cocktail glass is probably the most famous glass. It has been an emblem of high-class liquor for a long time. With a wide mouth, a conical saucer, and a long stem, which helps to keep the drink cold.

Manhattan or Rob Roy Cocktail

Rob Roy: **Named in honor of an operetta based upon Scottish folk hero Rob Roy Mcgregor. Created by a bartender from the Waldorf Astoria in Manhattan, New York City in 1894. The drink is similar to the Manhattan cocktail but replacing the Bourbon with Scotch.**

Ingredients:

2 oz of Scotch.

1 oz of sweet Vermouth.

2 or 3 dashes of bitters.

1. Add all the ingredients into a mixing glass over ice and stir.
2. Strain into a chilled cocktail glass.
3. Garnish with Maraschino cherries.

Old Fashioned: Developed around the 19th century. The recipe has changed with the years in some cases adding different liquors on top of the main spirit. On this interpretation, we will keep it simple.

Ingredients:

1 tsp of sugar.

2 oz of Bourbon or Rye Whiskey.

2 or 3 dashes of bitters.

1. In an Old Fashioned[18] glass, muddle the bitters and sugar.
2. Add the whiskey and fill it with ice.
3. Garnish with Orange Wheel and Maraschino Cherries.

Old Fashioned Cocktail

Irish Coffee: There are many recipes of coffee cocktails older than the famous Irish coffee. Several stories claim to be the origin of the drink. One of them mentions that Joe Sheridan head chef of a restaurant and coffee shop located in the airbase of town called Foynes in Ireland, invented the drink around 1943 and he served to the personal disembarking the planes. Another one claims that it was invented by Joseph Jackson around World War II, he made the drink to keep his fellow mates awake during German bombardments.

---

[18] Old Fashioned glass, often referred as rock glass or lowball glass. Is short and cylindrical with a tick base, primarily used for sipping drinks straight or with some ice.

Ingredients:
1 ½ oz of Irish Whiskey.
2 tsp of Brown Sugar.
Brewed hot coffee.

1. Fill an Irish coffee mug[19] with hot water and let it rest for 2 minutes, then discard the water.
2. Add the Whiskey and sugar, top with coffee and stir.
3. For garnish use unsweetened whip cream.

Irish Coffee - Image by grafmex from Pixabay

Mint Julep: The drink was created around the 18th century in the southern United States. The term julep originates from the Spanish word "julepe" a card game, from Spanish-Arabic, and this from the Persian word "Golab" (rosewater[20]).

Ingredients:
¼ oz Simple syrup[21].

---

[19] Irish coffee mug, is primarily used on cocktails related with coffee. It's made from clear glass and features a squat stem and base.

[20] Rosewater is a flavored water that is made by soaking roses petals in water and also by the distillation product of roses called hydrosol. Very popular in Europe and Asia for religious purposes.

[21] Some recipes might replace the simple syrup with sugar, honey, maple syrup and/or agave nectar.

8 Mint leaves.

2 oz of Bourbon.

1. In a highball[22] glass, lightly muddle the mint and the syrup.
2. Add the bourbon and fill with crushed ice.
3. Stir until the cup gets frosty outside.
4. Top with more crushed ice to form like a dome and garnish mint leaves.

Mint Julep

Rusty Nail: This cocktail showed up around the 1930s but it wasn't until the 1960s that it paved its name.

Ingredients:

---

[22] Highball glass name comes from a cocktail with the same name. Is tall and wide.

2 oz of blended Scotch Whisky.

½ oz of Drambuie[23] liqueur.

1. Combine all ingredients in an Old Fashioned glass, add one large ice cube and stir.
2. Garnish with a lemon twist.

Rusty Nail Cocktail

Enjoy and cheers!

---

[23] Drambuie is a liqueur made of Scotch whisky, honey, herbs and spices. Legend says it was created by Prince Charles Edward Stuart, who led a Scottish uprising in the 1740s against the British crown.

About the Author

Abrahan Reyes is a spirit connoisseur. He currently works as an IT Engineer in Austin, Texas.

Besides being a passionate drink researcher, he also enjoys watching baseball games and read comic books.

You can follow him on Facebook:
https://www.facebook.com/abrahan.reyes.14473/

References

Grigsby, Jordan. "Sour Mash vs Sweet Mash, Who's the Real Winner?" The ABV Network, 25 February 2019, https://www.abvnetwork.com/whiskey-corner/2019/2/25/whats-the-deal-with-sour-mash-vs-sweet-mash

Vinepair Staff. "Why Wine Is Aged In Oak. A History Lesson" Vinepair, https://vinepair.com/wine-101/wine-aged-oak-history-lesson/

Made How Staff. "Whiskey" How Products Are Made, http://www.madehow.com/Volume-2/Whiskey.html

Levey, Martin. "Babylonian Chemistry: A Study of Arabic and Second Millennium B.C. Perfumery", Osiris 12, p. 376-389. 1956.

Forbes, Robert James. "A short history of the art of distillation: from the beginnings up to the death of Cellier Blumenthal". Leiden, 1970.

Whisky.com Staff. "The Whisky Success Story" Whisky.com, https://www.whisky.com/history.html

O'Donnovan, John. "Annals of The Kingdom of Ireland", p.785, footnote for year 1405. Dublin, 1856.

Whiskyguide.com Staff. "The History of Whisky" The Whisky Guide, 2005, https://web.archive.org/web/20100125105734/http:/www.thewhiskyguide.com/Facts/History.html

Kosar, Kevin R. "What the Tea Party Could Learn from the Whiskey Rebellion" AlcoholReviews.com, 11 November 2010, http://alcoholreviews.com/2010/11/11/what-the-tea-party-could-learn-from-the-whiskey-rebellion/

Harrison, Joel. "Whisky in India" Live Mint, 29 December 2011, https://www.livemint.com/Companies/ny0g0a6Vo9Xz7DlB2TGcYI/Whisky-in-India.html

Whiskyfacts.com Staff. "Interesting Information about Whisky" Whisky Facts, http://www.whiskyfacts.com/

Shuster, Amanda. "How different grains affect the taste of your whiskey" Distiller Blog, 6 August 2017, https://blog.distiller.com/whiskey-grains/

Emen, Jake. "Understanding Whiskey Stills: Pots, Columns, Hybrids" The Whiskey Wash, 9 May 2016, https://thewhiskeywash.com/whiskey-styles/american-whiskey/understanding-whiskey-stills-pots-columns-hybrids/

Wikipedia Contributors. "Whisky" Wikipedia the free Encyclopedia, 19 September 2019, https://en.wikipedia.org/w/index.php?title=Whisky&oldid=916475075

Wikipedia Contributors. "Cereal" Wikipedia the free Encyclopedia, 4 November 2019, https://en.wikipedia.org/w/index.php?title=Cereal&oldid=924613805

Compound Interest Staff. "The Chemistry of Whisky" Compound Interest, 31 March 2015, https://www.compoundchem.com/2015/03/31/whisky/

The Whisky Exchange Staff. The Whisky Exchange. https://www.thewhiskyexchange.com/

Graham, Collen. "15 Essential Whiskey Cocktails Everyone Should Try The Sprice Eats", The Spruce Eats, 22 Oct 2019, https://www.thespruceeats.com/essential-whiskey-cocktails-761277

Liquor.com staff. "Recipe section" Liquor.com, https://www.liquor.com/

Bevvy staff. "Glassware" Bevvy, https://bevvy.co/glassware

Best, Katelyn. "Get Oat: Oats Have Been Used in Whiskey for Centuries" The Whiskey Wash, 8 May 2017, https://thewhiskeywash.com/lifestyle/get-oat-oats-used-whiskey-centuries/

Grier, Jacob. "Rise of rice whisky" Distiller Blog, 16 July 2017, https://blog.distiller.com/rice-whisky/

Emen, Jake. "Explore Whiskey Made From Alternative Grains" Whisky Advocate, 1 December 2016, http://whiskyadvocate.com/explore-whiskey-made-from-alternative-grains/

Difford, Simon. "Canadian Whisky" Difford's Guide, https://www.diffordsguide.com/beer-wine-spirits/category/563/canadian-whiskey

The Whiskey Wash staff. "Canadian Whisky: Things You Should Know From The Expert" The Whisky Wash, 5 November 2015, https://thewhiskeywash.com/whiskey-styles/canadian-whiskey/canadian-whisky-things-you-should-know-from-the-expert/

Johnston, Zach. "Here's How To Tell The Difference Between Bourbon And Tennessee Whiskey" Uproxx, 10 April 2019, https://uproxx.com/life/difference-between-kentucky-bourbon-and-tennessee-whiskey/

Lamb, Jess. "Is English Whisky a Thing" Winerist, 8 August 2018, https://www.winerist.com/magazine/drink/is-english-whisky-a-thing

Rail, Evans. "5 Stops on Germany's Whiskey Trail" The New York Times, 4 October 2019, https://www.nytimes.com/2019/10/04/travel/germany-whiskey.html

Barna, Maxwell. "8 Scientific Studies That Prove Whiskey is Good for You" Cool Material, https://coolmaterial.com/food-drink/health-benefits-whiskey/

Harvard T. H. Chan staff. "Alcohol: Balancing Risks and Benefits" Harvard School of Public Health, https://www.hsph.harvard.edu/nutritionsource/healthy-drinks/drinks-to-consume-in-moderation/alcohol-full-story/

Made in the USA
Monee, IL
08 February 2020